Marilyn Monroe:

The Live-In Housekeeper did it

….all of it,

independently,

and The Kennedy's

had nothing to do with it

By Investigative Author

Gwendolyn Olmsted

First published by Amazon.com October 2014

© Copyright 2014 Gwendolyn Olmsted

The moral right of the author has been asserted.

This book is licensed for your personal enjoyment only. This book may not be re-sold or given away to other people. No part of this book may be used or reproduced without written permission.

This book is a non-fictional research project; references are cited at the end of this book.

The scenario presented in this book is the most probable, based on the facts analyzed, yet the actual hand that led to the events that killed Marilyn Monroe, may never be known.

Book Class: True Crime

1st Edition: 1 October 2014

Available in paperback and *Kindle* ® e-book formats

Publisher: ***Amazon*** ®

© Copyright 2014 book cover design by Gwendolyn Olmsted

© Copyright 2014 cover photo used (circa 1956), was retrieved by snap-grab photo method from more than one source from the Internet 20 September 2014, listed in the References Section

© Copyright 2014 back photo used (circa 1940's), was retrieved by snap-grab photo method from more than one source from the Internet 20 September 2014, listed in the References Section

*The ***name*** of the high school teacher in Chapter One was changed, although the facts are real.

Table of Contents:

Marilyn Monroe: The Live-in Housekeeper did it

Summary
Prelude
Prologue

Chapter 1
Chapter 2
Chapter 3
Chapter 4
Chapter 5
Chapter 6
Chapter 7
Chapter 8
Chapter 9
Chapter 10
Chapter 11

References
Postscript
About the Author

Summary

The untimely death of one of the most recognized faces who had ever graced Hollywood, Marilyn Monroe, has led to more than one theory surrounding her unsolved departure from the world, the causes, what lead up to it, and contrary to popular belief, The Kennedy's had nothing to do with the death of Marilyn Monroe.

It was the live-in housekeeper, Eunice Murray, whose hand, acting alone, and independently, killed Marilyn, in her sleep, while she was tranquilizing in the seclusion and solitude of her own bedroom in the early evening of August 4th, 1962. Even up until the very day Eunice died in March 1994, no one had ever interviewed her even once .... as a potential suspect.

Marilyn Monroe: The Live-in Housekeeper did it, exploits the evidence and reasoning that points to how and why live-in housekeeper, Eunice Murray, who acting alone, and independently stole the life of perhaps the greatest screen siren of the twentieth century: Marilyn Monroe.

Prelude

Hollywood is a place where they'll pay you

a thousand dollars for a kiss

and fifty cents for your soul.

~Marilyn Monroe, circa 1950

Prologue

It was actually in 1983, when I learned the true cause of death of Marilyn Monroe. I was taking a film course at an upper middle class public high school within the confines of Los Angeles County, California, in the white Jewish suburbs, in the upper quarter of the northwest county quadrant. All of the students there had parents who were overly-gainfully employed in some sort of faction throughout the inner corridors of the movie industry, and what an onerous footing that was to find yourself on the *inside* of those colossal, massive, thundering, heavy solid doors used to keep hopefuls out, called Hollywood-land .
Although there were a few students with parents of famous actors and actresses, and a handful of child actors and actresses at that, most of these people had parents who worked ***behind*** the scenes: Screen writers, script writers, sit-com writers, game show writers, game show hosts, news anchors, studio accountants, studio executives, studio lawyers, directors, producers, agents, cameramen, photographers, animators, voice-overs, and of course, don't leave out the forefathers of this wholesome and kosher industry of make-believe, the has-beens, who have had over a hundred movies to their names, yet no one can remember who the Hell they ever were.
At the age of seventeen, which was the age I was in

1983, while conquering eleventh grade, that was pretty much how it worked in the hamlet I called home, up until I reached the age of majority, less than one year later.

Chapter 1

As I sat in my classroom of fourth period Film Studies class, the class right before lunch, but then I was an American girl, and I never ate lunch in high school. Anorexic? No, but this was the 1980's, and I strived to be successful, so I certainly did try to be, standing 5'10", weighing 140 pounds. Boy was I fat, I thought of myself. Actually I wasn't fat at all, and didn't have one once of fat on my entire body, but this was America, and I am a girl, so high school ……. was pretty physically painful.

Furthermore, my best friend since fourth grade, Ramona Lestak, had told everyone I was a lesbian after she said she wouldn't be my friend anymore unless I les-ed off with her, had somehow convinced the entire school I was gay, of which I never was gay, ever. I les-ed off with her in eighth grade, like she had threatened or end our friendship, then she said she didn't want to be my friend anymore anyway, so from ninth grade onward, I was known as the class lesbian, because of her lies.

Funny to look back at now: I had my birth control all taken care of in my overly fertile earthly architecture: Abstinence, not by choice, although I always was puzzled at how I was never able to be with the boyfriend who should have been mine: Rick. This of course I found out years later.

In walked my teacher for this film studies class, named Joshua Lowenstein, about as Jewish as you could possibly get. He said he came from a long line of people who were employed in every aspect of Hollywood imaginable.

He also told everyone he was teaching instead of continuing that Hollywood tradition on, because his dad had died, and without connections, I guess you have nothing…. in an industry like the industry Hollywood is.

This was not the first day of the semester, spring semester, yet as he walked up to the front of the class, he started writing on the chalk board, with real actual chalk, yes this was the 1980's, the name:

MARILYN MONROE

"Can anyone tell me anything they know about Marilyn Monroe?"

"Norma Jean Baker." One classmate said.

"President Kennedy's mistress," said another.

"… and one of several, right?" this eleventh grade high school teacher joked.

They wanted a good grade in his class, so they all laughed, but then it *was* pretty funny too.

"The most famous person in all of Hollywood?" stated another student.

"….actually that would be Charlie Chaplin, but close enough." The teacher informed.

"Slept with every single man she ever met," stated another still.

"Can anyone tell me how she died?" asked the teacher.

Stone silence. All the joking had stopped, and the class just looked around the room and stared at each other.

"It was undetermined.." I piped up. I was quite shy in high school, which probably explains why and how I am just the opposite in ways now, yet just had to say that.

Joshua looked over at me, yet said nothing. He had all the students call him by his first name, the only teacher in school who did.

"It was ruled a suicide," said a girl, sadly.

"It was the Kennedy's who iced her," a football looking young man declared.

"Actually, it was her live-in house-keeper who did it," the teacher projected.

"Why?" someone asked.

"Marilyn had given her a pink slip two weeks earlier, terminating her employment with her, stating she had two weeks to vacate her residence, and the day Marilyn died, would have been her last day working there under her employ," Joshua informed a bewildered class of upper middle class students.

"Eunice Murray: .... and to this day, she has never been considered a suspect," he said.

"Why don't they arrest her?.... or question her?" I asked so curious, I temporarily forgot I was shy, and placed an inquiry in just like I was an adult already over the age of eighteen.

"Why don't they *indeed*?" he repeated the question to the class.

"How do *you* know all this?" stated a member of student government who undoubtedly grew up to be an attorney.

"I know all the ins and outs of Hollywood, every faucet, every crevice, every loophole you can, and cannot possibly comprehend, that's how I know; growing up in and around **all** the inner circles of Hollywood tends to lend you an extra ear, an ear not available or accessible to the general public ……. or apparently not even to the government." Joshua Lowenstein stated, while laughing, all proud of himself.

I started to focus around myself, because I had been daydreaming of my days in high school, it now being 2014, and I was a far cry from seventeen anymore. Oh, if only I could turn back the clock and do it all over again….. except differently, in every possible way, differently.

Today, I am an investigative reporter, who gets paid, as I go… a good story means a hefty payload; and a dull dreary story means, Kraft ® macaroni and cheese for dinner.

The fascination with the death of Marilyn Monroe: It still haunts us today.

She was a foster child, her mother too mentally ill to care for her, not even knowing who her real dad was, and had one failed marriage after another: Marilyn, or Norma Jean had every reason in the world to kill herself.

Yet, reports, outlier reports, including the reference from my eleventh grade film studies teacher, who actually had a Master's degree from USC—*The University of Southern California Film Studies School*, proposed otherwise. I guess his dad must have died shortly *after* he had graduated. USC was and continues to be pretty expensive.

Chapter 2

In the wee hours of the morning of August 5th, 1962, in her west Los Angeles home located at 12305 Fifth Helena Drive, in Brentwood, California, lying in a prone position, with her face angled off to the left while on top of a pillow, she lay in a soldier's position: That's how the first law enforcement official who arrived on the scene described her position, immediately instinctively getting the feeling someone had placed her like that. Her legs were straight, together and fully extended, with her right arm straight against her body and fully extended, as well. Her left hand raised up over her head, yet off to the right, was clutching the receiver to a phone.

Of course, there were empty "sleeping pill" bottles specifically prescribed to *Marilyn Monroe* all over the room. Look and sound set up and staged? Perhaps it was, but not nearly by the people you may think, or were led by to think.

Autopsies later determined she had died of an overdose of barbiturates that had been introduced into her system by way of her large intestine, by way of an enema.

Large traces of Chloral hydrate were also found in lab reports from the autopsy. Chloral hydrate significantly slows down the metabolism of Nembutal, one of many prescribed drugs Marilyn was addicted to, yet was trying to stop taking. Dr. Greenson, her psychiatrist at the time, had been trying to break Marilyn's Nembutal habit and switched her to chloral hydrate as a sleep aid. However, Marilyn had various sources of her favorite drug and had plenty of them around her residence.

Nembutal and chloral hydrate interacted adversely together, something Marilyn did not know, nor would admit to the still taking of the Nembutal.

This combination of narcotics, would slowly render Marilyn to be in a "drugged out," condition, as her close friend Peter Lawford described her, when he called her at 7:45 p.m. to re-invite her over for a card party and dinner on the day she died. Although it was not the first time he had called her that day from his Malibu beach house to invite her over.

Based on the facts, she probably died at 8:00 p.m. that same day, since Eunice Murray's story has changed so many times, she, based on today's standards, would be considered incompetent by a court of law in 2014. But then she is the identified murderer in this version of the life and times of Marilyn Monroe, so would she come across as any other way?

If it were suicide, like it was officially determined, how could she possibly have given herself an enema……. of anything to herself? ……especially under those conditions.

Perhaps, the only time in history, where the notoriety of a person's stardom actually inhibited a murder investigation, was the case of the murder of Marilyn Monroe. A troubled life, a heart-breaking life, a lonely life, yet a sexually fulfilling life she led. She had no inhibitions like the rest of us have. She took what she wanted and left behind no moral or ethical remorse about her sexual exploits, about anything.

There was no formal coroner's inquest into Monroe's death in 1962, because the death appeared to be a suicide at first glance, prior to the conclusion of the autopsy.

The main investigative agency handling the case was the Los Angeles County coroner's office, then run by Dr. Theodore J. Curphey. Instead of conducting a public inquest, Dr. Curphey decided to appoint a three-member team of mental health professionals to probe into Monroe's background. Their report, which concluded that her death was a probable suicide, was issued eleven days later.

Maybe it was Marilyn's exceptional and super-human sexuality that although catapulted her to the top in life, had actually worked against her in death. No *proper* man taxed more time than was absolutely needed on the likes of Marilyn Monroe, even a dead Marilyn Monroe.

Interviews with Marilyn before her death revealed a less desperate, non-hysterical Marilyn as so many have described her.

Concerning the John and Robert Kennedy brother's triangle: Although she loved John Kennedy after engaging in sex with him, it was Robert, his brother, of whom she also engaged in shameless sex with as well, who was in love with *her*; isn't that just how life works?

As for the president's brother, Robert F. Kennedy, the U.S. attorney general at the time: "As you see, there is no room in my life for him. I guess I don't have the courage to face up to it and hurt him. I want someone else to tell him it's over. I tried to get the president to do it, but I couldn't reach him," Marilyn was quoted as saying in *Los Angeles Times* staff writer, Robert W. Welkos's, *New Chapter in the Mystery of Marilyn: Her Own Words?*, written in August 5th, 2005, one of the many auto-biographies about her, *after* her death, of course.
[Source Reference Number (13)].

Furthermore, and more on point, in the transcripts, Marilyn said she needed her current psychiatrist, Dr. Greenson's help in getting her housekeeper, Eunice Murray another job.

"Doctor, I want you to help me get rid of Murray.... I can't flat out fire her. Next thing would be a book 'Secrets of Marilyn Monroe by Her Housekeeper.' She'd make a fortune spilling what she knows and she knows too damn much," again Marilyn was quoted as saying, in her own actual words, by the same source. [Source Reference Number (13)].

Chapter 3

Norma Jeane Mortenson was born at 9:30 a.m. on June 1, 1926, at Los Angeles General Hospital, actually today know as *County University of Southern California Medical Center*, to Gladys Pearl Monroe Baker. Norma Jeane's dad was listed as Edward Mortenson on her birth certificate, yet it was unlikely that he was actually her biological dad. According to Donald H. Wolfe in *The Last Days of Marilyn Monroe,* Norma Jeane's biological father was Stanley Gifford. Stanley and Gladys worked together as film cutters for Consolidation Film Industries, where a brief relationship allegedly developed between the two. However, by the time Gladys realized she was pregnant, Stanley Gifford had moved on to less burdensome activities.

Although the then Norma Jeane had an older half-brother and half-sister, because her mother was eventually placed in a mental institution when Marilyn was just seven, there was doubt she even knew of their existence. Her childhood was filled with disappointment, and more foster care families than could be kept track of. She even claimed she was sexually assaulted prior to her eighteenth birthday by one of the many encounters she came across in her multiple homes she found herself in.

Following Norma Jeane's later transformation to Marilyn Monroe, she was quoted as saying about her youth, "The world around me then was kind of grim. I had to learn to pretend in order to...I don't know...block the grimness. The whole world seemed sort of closed to me... I felt on the outside of everything and all I could do was to dream up any kind of pretend game," stated Rachel Bell in her article on Marilyn Monroe from *The Crime Library* [Source reference Number (7)].

On June 19, 1942, Jim Dougherty and Norma Jeane were legally married, mostly because she had nowhere else to go, and Jim was a neighbor who needed a wife. Norma Jeane was barely sixteen, when she wed her very first husband, what would wind up being one of three. Although the marriage was one of convenience, she earnestly tried in the beginning to be a good wife and housekeeper. "The good wife" role was one Marilyn never meshed into: It just wasn't in her nature.

In 1943, Jim joined the Merchant Marines and a year later he was shipped off to New Guinea and then to the Pacific during World War II. To fill the time and to make money, Norma Jeane worked at an aircraft and parachute-inspecting plant named *Radio Plane*

Munitions Factory, where she inspected and painted planes. However, the job did little to ease her boredom and she grew increasingly lonely and insecure during her husband's absence.

In mid-1944, Norma Jeane was offered an exciting break and a way to escape her boring life: An army photographer named Private David Conover was doing a piece for *Yank* magazine on women at work for the war effort, when he spotted the overly loving and natural beauty of Norma Jeane. Conover paid her $5 an hour to model for him for several weeks, and the two traveled around southern California on a photo shooting session. The pictures were quickly produced and it wasn't long before she gained her first modeling contract with *the Blue Book Model Agency*.

By 1945, Norma Jeane's popularity skyrocketed and she appeared on the covers of over thirty national magazines. Her modeling career quickly became a success.

By the time her first husband returned home from overseas, in the summer of 1946, they divorced: September 13th, 1946. Although, after being gone that long, despite Marilyn's successes, a marriage like that would have ended in divorce regardless, even during that era. It is just human nature, with an extended absence like that, especially considering the circumstances in which they were married under.

On August 26, 1946, Marilyn signed a seventy-five dollar a week contract to act for *Twentieth Century Fox*, after an interview with Ben Lyon. It was for six months, and she was twenty years old. It was at this time, with the persuasion of studio executives, that her name was changed to Marilyn Monroe.

Almost one year to the day she signed her contract, *Twentieth Century Fox* dropped Marilyn Monroe with no explanation. Marilyn was just as quickly out of cash as she was out of a job. Marilyn took this opportunity to become involved in the Actors Laboratory, which was an off Broadway talent transplanted in Los Angeles.

In *Marilyn Monroe: The Biography,* Donald Spoto states that this exposure to the controversial and intellectual characters of New York theater and accomplished actors had lent a certain level of refinement to Marilyn, one she had not encountered up to that point in her entire life. Yet at this same time in her life, she had also begun soft-pornography, and modeling for over-the-top sexuality calendars that the camera seemed to capture every time she stepped in front of it.

In March 1948, Marilyn signed another six month contract, this one with *Columbia Pictures*, paying as well, seventy-five dollars a week. It was Marilyn's sexual relationship with seventy-year-old Joe Schenck, one of the founders of *Twentieth Century Fox Motion Pictures Studios* that had opened this door for her. Because of this however, precisely six months after the contract was signed, it was terminated.

Later in 1948, Marilyn began another sexual relationship with one of Hollywood's most influential and powerful agents, Johnny Hyde, age fifty-five.

It was in fact Hollywood agent Johnny Hyde that credits Marilyn's physical transformation to the Marilyn Monroe image to that which we all know today.

Hollywood agent Johnny Hyde convinced Marilyn to have plastic surgery on her chin to remove scars, regularly bleach her hair and, to have her tubes tied so that she was unable to have children. Marilyn up to that point had more than one abortion from previous lovers, as well as miscarriages, slowing her work, as well as emotional state down. This was something the studios could not have.

Hollywood agent Johhny Hyde also assisted Marilyn in obtaining a contract with the company that had two years earlier turned her away: *Twentieth Century Fox*. Except this time she was paid five hundred dollars a week for her role in the movie *Asphalt Jungle,* her first serious movie role.

Her next movie was one that shaped the character we know her as today: *All About Eve*. Marilyn began to receive great reviews for her performances and her image as a sex symbol was instigated. In Kirk Wilson's book about Marilyn Monroe, cinematographer Leon Shamroy stated what many men felt when they saw Marilyn in a movie: He got the chills when he saw Marilyn on screen and that, "She had a kind of fantastic beauty in which she was actually able to put sex on a piece of film."

In December 1950, Hollywood agent Johnny Hyde died of a myocardial infarction, thus ending his relationship with Marilyn, both sexually, yet professionally too.

Chapter 4

It was this loss that caused Marilyn to try to kill herself by overdosing on an entire bottle of sleeping pills. Her roommate and drama coach called for an ambulance, and she received medical treatment at a hospital, and lived another day. This was well covered in the media and press: Everyone knew Marilyn had tried to commit suicide, and the method in which she chose: Downing a bottle of sleeping pills.

In 1951, Marilyn signed another six month contract with *Fox Studios*, and because of her ability to bring in the dollar, was later turned into a seven year contract.

In 1951, Marilyn met playwright Arthur Miller, who would be her third husband, but not yet.

1952 was Marilyn's most successful year, professionally, with the making of what wound up being her two best movies, *Niagara* and *Gentlemen Prefer Blondes*. Yet they were both released in 1953.

On January 14th, 1954, one year after dating, Marilyn and Yankees baseball legend Joe DiMaggio were wed less than two weeks after Marilyn's suspension, one of many from *Fox Studios,* in San Francisco, California.

On October 27th, 1954, at Marilyn's initiation, they were divorced. Joe wanted a woman that was married to just him, not the entire world, and showed that to Marilyn in numerous jealous rages. Yet his obsession and love for Marilyn never faded up until the day he died. Upon Marilyn's death, Joe made all the funeral arrangements, and he sent flowers to her grave every day until shortly before his own death on March 8th, 1999.

Throughout 1955 and 1956, Marilyn moved in with some friends in Connecticut, and later into an apartment in New York City. It was during this time that she opened up her own studio called *Marilyn Monroe Productions*, with the help of Milton Greene. Several successful movies were released under the studio's name, as well as more continued movies from Marilyn's long standing relationship with *Twentieth Century Fox.*

This caught the attention of playwright Arthur Miller, and on June 29th, 1956, Arthur Miller and Marilyn were married. Because intellect and beauty apparently clashed in this relationship, they divorced in 1961. The marriage lasted four and a half years, and would later turn out to be Marilyn's longest marriage.

It was a curious marriage indeed after researching Arthur Miller's character: He was cold; reserved; un-loving; devoted to his profession of play writing and book authoring of the most serious of subjects; Jewish and knew exactly where he came from to the point where I think he resented it. And Marilyn, the opposite in every possible way: Whimsical; playful; naïve; childlike; a child of the world, since what little she knew of her past, she tried her hardest to forget it, to forget the pain.

From 1961 up until her death in mid-1962, Marilyn seemed to be employed exclusively by the psychiatric community of the day, which lived by the theory: Lobotomize or "drug out." Marilyn chose, or had chosen for her, to "drug out," and lived the rest of her days, approximately six-hundred since divorcing Arthur Miller in 1961, of them either stoned from prescription medication or alcohol.

And although she only took drugs prescribed to her, she also battled severe addictions to barbiturates and alcohol. Her treating psychiatrist from 1961 until her death was Dr. Ralph Greenson. He would be the last psychiatrist to ever professionally treat Marilyn.

Although she continued to work in Hollywood, on the set of *Something's Got to Give*, to be exact, her erratic behavior and chemical addictions caused her to give other goals a top priority, even over her chosen line of work as a movie star.

Chapter 5

In 1961, her social life gained a top spot in Marilyn's daily activities, and she befriended several high-profile personalities during that time, including Peter Lawford, who happened to be the husband of Pat Kennedy, current President John F. Kennedy's sister, and their friends became hers. The entire group often spent time together, frequently attending gatherings or large parties at the Lawford and Kennedy homes. The guests were the who's who of not only the Hollywood crowd, but also the Washington DC scene as well. At times high government officials attended, including Robert Kennedy and his brother, then President John Kennedy. According to Tim Coates' *Marilyn Monroe: The F.B.I Files*, it was during these parties that Marilyn and the Kennedy brothers, both, developed sexual relationships with Marilyn, during the beginning months of 1962.

According to friends of Marilyn, who at times told so many lies and fantasies as if they were true, being in the "drugged-out" and drunken stupors she lived in the remaining year and a half of her life, a reported sexual relationship developed between Marilyn and the two Kennedy brothers. She was believed to have had separate affairs with the two men simultaneously.

Her relationships with Robert and John, became the talk of the Hollywood community; although, the Washington DC crowd didn't much care. To the upper classes, what most politicians were until recently, Hollywood was considered "scum," and unworthy of even engaging in conversation over. It is a completely different world today. Marilyn was often seen dancing or in intimate conversation at private parties with Bobby or John. However, according to her closest friends, her true love was then President of the United States of America, John.

Over the years, the FBI obtained information on Marilyn because some of her friends were Communists, and the belief was that Marilyn might be one too. But later, the FBI retained an interest in Marilyn because of her sexual relationship with the President of the United States, and was growing an ever-increasing file on her activities.

Because of her at least "said" sexual involvement with John and Robert Kennedy, whether true or not, criminal organizations, such as the Mafia took an interest in Marilyn as well, although the extent may never be known.

In 1962, Marilyn moved into a house, a Mexican style bungalow in Brentwood, California, in West Los Angeles closer to Malibu, from her previous apartment located more toward the heart of Los Angeles. She purposely moved to be close to the Lawford Malibu beach house where she was increasingly spending more and more of her time, but also closer to her psychiatrist, Dr. Ralph Greenson, whom she eventually began seeing on a daily basis. Marilyn's depression and anxieties began to worsen because of her increased prescription drug use, caused by her severe mismanagement by Dr. Ralph Greenson's methods. During these last six-hundred days of her life, Marilyn overdosed on sleeping pills and had to have her stomach pumped for drugs often. If this happened today, Dr. Ralph Greenson would have had his medical license revoked. But is wasn't 2014; the years were 1961 and 1962.

So, what did Marilyn do? She became increasingly dependent on Dr. Greenson and continuously consulted with him on her out-of-control life: Just the thing to guarantee patient loyalty, especially a rich and famous one. One can never have too many rich and famous patients. Taking care of Marilyn became a full-time job for her psychiatrist and he strongly

suggested she hire a live-in housekeeper ……..
named Eunice Murray.

According to reports, live-in housekeeper Eunice Murray performed many duties for Marilyn including driving her to and from Dr, Greenson's home and office in Santa Monica, secretarial and nursing duties. and cleaning her house. She also monitored Marilyn's activities and kept track of her behavior and moods, which she, in the end, reported to Dr. Greenson daily. Marilyn's friends noticed Eunice Murray and Dr. Greenson were unusually involved in every aspect of Marilyn's life from the moment she first met him.

It should be noted that Marilyn Monroe began seeing Dr. Greenson as one of his patients, as a result of her divorce from her longest marriage to Arthur Miller, which was shortly *before* her involvement in political interests, like the President of the United States of America.,

In 1962, Marilyn's relationship peaked with the Kennedy's brothers Robert and then current President John. Marilyn was often seen in the company of either John or Robert Kennedy. It was believed that Bobby fell in love with Marilyn, but she did not reciprocate his feelings, although she cared for him deeply and had maintained a sexual relationship with him.

Marilyn's friends agreed that her heart was set on winning the affections of John F. Kennedy. He began seeing her often, either at her home or at the Lawford's beach house in Malibu.

On one occasion they were caught by a former Kennedy advisor, Peter Summers, who saw them come out from the bathroom together. Marilyn was wearing just a towel. Summers was quoted as saying, "She had clearly been in there, in the shower, with him. It was obvious, but neither of them seemed worried about it." This was substantial, because it indicated that the Kennedy brother's were not privatizing their sexual exploits with Marilyn at all; to the contrary, they were showing them off, to anyone willing to watch.

The Lawford home was not the only place where Marilyn and John exacerbated each other's sexuality with one another. Marilyn and John also meet during Kennedy's travels as The President, and met where ever they felt like it.

Marilyn Monroe and John F. Kennedy were two personas who took whatever they wanted from the world without a shred of regard for who they hurt or what consequences they evoked. Did Marilyn Monroe and The then President of the United States John F. Kennedy have sex and sexual encounters? Absolutely.

John also spoke frequently to Marilyn on the phone beginning in 1962. He even gave her a private number so that she could call him through the Justice Department. Marilyn was lead to believe at this time that John F. Kennedy and she would be Mr. and Mrs. President of the United States of America and that he would divorce his wife Jackie soon, and marry her: Marilyn began to imagine herself as a future First Lady.

This was during an era when *all* young women in the United States shared that same fantasy: The 1960's.

Since the Clinton Administration, in the 1990's, the title of "First Lady," is now not a very desired one.

As far as the sexual relationship with Robert Kennedy, although most people involved during the day say there was a sexual relationship between them,

I find it highly unlikely, given the large number of children Robert Kennedy had with his wife and because of his high moral values he had as the United States Attorney General.

Chapter 6

In 1962, Marilyn Monroe began filming *Something's Got to Give,* which was to be the third film of her four-film contract with *Twentieth Century Fox*. It co-starred Dean Martin and Cyd Charisse. However, Marilyn's heath was quite compromised with either a bacterial infection or virus onset, at the start of this project. When she returned to health, on one occasion she refused to perform with Dean Martin just because he had a cold. Producer Henry Weinstein recalled seeing her on several occasions being physically ill as she prepared to film her scenes, and attributed it to her dread of performing. He commented, "Very few people experience terror. We all experience anxiety, unhappiness, heartbreaks, but that was sheer primal terror." [Source Reference Number (16): Wikipedia.org].

On May 19, 1962, she attended the early birthday celebration of President John F. Kennedy at Madison Square Garden, at the suggestion of Kennedy's brother-in-law, actor Peter Lawford. Monroe sang "Happy Birthday" along with a specially written verse based on Bob Hope's "Thanks for the Memory". John F. Kennedy responded to her performance in such a condescending was, with the remark, "Thank you. I can now retire from politics after having had 'Happy Birthday' sung to me in such a sweet, wholesome way." [Source Reference Number (16): Wikipedia.org].

In the summer of 1962, Marilyn had become a security risk and was told to cease all contact with the President of the United States, and his Attorney General brother. The relationships came to an abrupt end and Marilyn was shattered.

But in the weeks just before Marilyn's death, her career and personal life were in a definite upswing. There were a number of new valuable film projects that she was working on and she was very excited about being involved in these new money-making projects.

There was also the weekend before she died that was spent at Lake Tahoe. She spent that weekend with Joe DiMaggio and that they planned to remarry.

However, others claim that Frank Sinatra had set up the weekend at the Cal-Neva Lodge at the request of the Kennedys who wanted to make sure that Marilyn did not leak to the press the details of her relationship with the President. These proved to be propaganda for the newspapers to write about.

The reality of it was: DiMaggio came to Tahoe unexpectedly and arrived late Saturday night, perhaps because Marilyn asked him to come. Furthermore, research indicated that mafia kingpin Sam Giancana was also there to ensure that Marilyn did not create a problem for the Kennedys.

DiMaggio was furious with Sinatra and the Kennedys for luring Marilyn there, pumping her up with her own drugs and then taking compromising photos of her to be used as blackmail if she threatened to expose the Kennedys love affair with her, which doesn't make any sense, since Marilyn already had plenty of those lying around.

The following weekend Marilyn was found dead in her West Los Angeles house. Her death appeared to be a suicide resulting from an overdose of sleeping pills. However, there were many who believed that she was murdered because she simply knew too much. And some even believe her live-in housekeeper, Eunice Murray, did the final deed, fed up with Marilyn's shenanigans, and of her day-dreaming of being a future first lady. After all, that wouldn't be the first time a man in history has given it all away over love.

Look at the case of the British Monarchy, when King Edward VIII did something that monarchs do not have the luxury of doing - he fell in love. Edward VIII (1894-1972) became King of England upon the death of his father, George V, on January 20, 1936.

However, shortly afterwards, Edward made known his desire to marry an American woman named Wallis Warfield Simpson, whom he had known since 1931. He sought the approval of his family, the Church of England, and the political establishment to marry her, but met with strong opposition. She had been married twice before and her second divorce was still pending.

The love affair and possible royal marriage resulted in sensational newspaper headlines around the world and created a storm of controversy, but did not sway Edward. On December 10, 1936, King Edward VIII submitted his abdication and it was endorsed by Parliament the next day. He thus became the only British monarch ever to resign voluntarily.

His younger brother, George VI, took the throne and immediately gave Edward the title, Duke of Windsor. The Duke and Simpson were married in France on June 3, 1937 and lived in Paris. During World War II, Edward served as governor of the Bahamas. He died in Paris on May 28, 1972. His wife died there, April 24, 1986. **[Source Reference Number (21)]**

To some, this was the love story of the century. To others, it was a scandal that threatened to weaken the monarchy. In reality, the story of King Edward VIII and Mrs. Wallis Simpson never fulfilled either of these notions. It was just about a man of power, and a very influential woman, looked at by the Monarchy, as "scum," who fell in love with each other, and would do anything to keep it.

There are also countless other stories where US Senators, while away in Washington DC with their wives back home in whatever state they are from, take up a girlfriend, or mistress, that causes them to divorce their wife and marry their Washington DC girlfriend. There are too many to count.

Love like that is real: Sometimes it really does evolve into a new marriage for the exploring, or rather lonely man with his "other woman," something Marilyn was called a lot of.

Marilyn very well could have been a First Lady under the Kennedy Administration, and the sun would have continued to rise and set every day… still. And furthermore, during that era of the 1960's what woman did not daydream about becoming First Lady of the United States of America?

Eunice was enraged with jealousy. "Marilyn can't do that," Eunice thought. "She is severely mentally ill, and she needs to stay that way or I won't have a job any longer, and neither will Dr. Ralph Greenson," were some of the things racing through Eunice's own mind in the days leading up to Marilyn's death.

The issue in not whether Marilyn had a real chance at marrying President John F. Kennedy. The issue is that she believed she did, and maybe her obsessive talk about it, either caused unsurmountable jealousy in Eunice Murray, or maybe the fact that the day Marilyn died was supposed to be Eunice Murray's last day working for Marilyn, as indicated by a pink slip she was given two weeks prior, and was reminded of more than once throughout August 4th, 1962, the day Eunice Murray killed Marilyn Monroe.

Chapter 7

Timeline:
[Source Reference Number (8): *Wikipedia.org*]

Many questions remain unanswered regarding the circumstances and timeline of Monroe's death after her body was found. Many elements of this timeline have often been brought into question. Most notable are the discrepancies in exactly what time Marilyn either made or received her last phone call and at what time during the late night and early morning hours of August 4 and 5 her body was discovered.

- **~5:00 p.m.**: Marilyn's personal psychiatrist, Dr. Ralph Greenson, leaves her Brentwood house after another session in one of many strategic attempts to treat her ongoing depression.

- **~7:15 p.m.**: Joe DiMaggio Jr., son of baseball player Joe DiMaggio (and thus Monroe's former stepson) phones her about his broken engagement to a girl in San Diego. DiMaggio Jr. said when interviewed that Monroe sounded cheerful and upbeat. On duty with the Marines at Marine Corps Base Camp Pendleton 97 miles southeast of Monroe's home, DiMaggio was able to place the time of the call because he was watching the seventh inning of a Baltimore Orioles-Los Angeles Angels game being played in Baltimore. According to the game's records the seventh inning took place between 10 and 10:15 p.m. Eastern Daylight Time; thus, Monroe received the call around 7 p.m. California time.

- ~7:45 p.m.: Peter Lawford telephones Monroe to invite her to dinner at his house, an invitation she declined earlier that day. According to Peter Lawford's later statements, Monroe's speech is slurred and is becoming increasingly indecipherable. After telling him goodbye the conversation abruptly ends. Peter Lawford tries to call her back again but receives a busy signal. Existing telephone records show that this is the last phone call Monroe's main line received that night.

- 7:55 p.m.: Taking advantage of Marilyn's increasingly near paralyzing condition from the Chloral Hydrate Dr. Greenson had given her earlier in the day, as well as the Nembutal that Marilyn probably took while no one was watching, Eunice Murray uses the key to enter Marilyn's bedroom (she had it all along) and before Marilyn had a chance to turn around, Eunice shoved an entire handful of Marilyn's "sleeping pills," or barbiturates up her rectum: Jealous over Marilyn's turning her life around; resentful over being a "servant" to Marilyn; hurt, angry, and humiliated over being given a pink slip for notice of termination of employment two weeks prior, and guess what! The day Marilyn died was to be Eunice's last day of employment with her.

- **~8:00 p.m.**: Marilyn most probably died immediately after Eunice's brutal attack.

- **~9:00 p.m.**: Peter Lawford (President Kennedy's brother-in-law) telephones Eunice Murray, spending the night in Monroe's guest house, on a different line asking if Eunice Murray would check in on her. After a few *seconds* Murray returns to the phone telling Peter Lawford that she is fine. Unconvinced, Peter Lawford will try all night long to get in touch with Marilyn. Peter Lawford telephones his friend and lawyer Milton A. "Mickey" Rudin, but is advised to keep away from Monroe's house to avoid any public embarrassment that could result from Monroe possibly being under the influence.

- **10:00 p.m.**: Housekeeper Eunice Murray walks past Monroe's bedroom door and later testifies that she saw a light on under the door but decided not to disturb Monroe.

- **12:00 a.m.**: Murray notices the light under the door again and knocks several times but gets no reply.

- **1:00 a.m.**: Peter Lawford is informed by Mickey Rudin that Monroe is dead. He informs Peter Lawford that it was an overdose.

- **3:00 a.m.**: Eunice Murray calls Marilyn's personal psychiatrist, Dr. Greenson, on the second telephone line, she still cannot awake Marilyn. She is sure something is very wrong after peeking into her barred bedroom window.

- **3:40 a.m.**: Dr. Greenson arrives and tries to break open the door but fails. It was just a regular bedroom door. Why would he not be able to break it down? …. unless he was trying to stage a crime scene. He looks through the French windows outside and sees Marilyn lying on the bed holding the telephone and apparently dead, so he breaks the glass to open the locked door and checks her. He calls Dr. Hyman Engelberg. There is some speculation that an ambulance might have been summoned to Monroe's house at this point and later dismissed.

- Eunice needed all witnesses and interested parties—apparently the entire world, to know she did not have access to Marilyn's room. That was the one significant vital evidence Eunice always fell back on: "I never had the key to Marilyn's room." She couldn't have: She would have implicated herself for sure then. She would have no more tricks to hide had anyone known she had the key to Marilyn's personal room.

- Eunice Murray was assigned at the "strong and severe suggestion" of Dr. Ralph Greenson to watch over and tend to Marilyn Monroe as her assigned housekeeper, driver, and doorwoman: Yes, Eunice Murray most definitely did have the key to Marilyn's bedroom, if one ever existed.

- Would it not have been easier to bang the door down than bust open the window, shattering glass everywhere? Yes, it would have, but Eunice needed everyone involved to know, she wanted that planted in their brains and hard-saved, that EUNICE MURRAY NEVER HAD ACCESS TO MARILYN MONROE THROUGH HER BEDROOM DOOR. That had to be embedded in their brains, or people would piece together that Eunice Murray, acting alone and independently had killed Marilyn Monroe. The Kennedy's had nothing to do with it, and never did.

- It should be noted that other reports on this crime scene indicated that Marilyn Monroe's bedroom door did not have an installed lock on it, so there never was a key to begin with.

- **4:30 a.m.**: Police are called and arrive shortly after. The two doctors and housekeeper Eunice Murray are questioned and indicate a time of death of around 12:30 a.m. **Police note the room is extremely tidy and the bed appears to have fresh linen on it. They claim Eunice Murray was washing sheets when they arrived.** Police note that the bedside table has several pill bottles but the room contains no means to wash pills down with because there is no glass and the water is turned off. Monroe is known to gag on pills even when drinking to wash them down. Later a glass is found lying on the floor by the bed but police claim it was not there when the room was initially searched upon arrival.

- **5:40 a.m.**: Undertaker Guy Hockett arrives and notes that the state of rigor mortis indicates a time of death between 9:30 and 11:30 p.m. The time is later altered to match the witness statements.

- **6:00 a.m.**: Eunice Murray changes her story and now says she went back to bed at midnight and only called Dr. Greenson when she awoke at 3 a.m. and noticed the light still on. Both doctors also change their stories and now claim Monroe died around 3:50 a.m. Police note that Eunice Murray appears quite evasive and extremely vague and she would eventually change her story several times. Despite being a key witness.

- Eunice Murray travels to Europe and is not questioned again…… ever. Although The Kennedy's had nothing to do with the murder of Marilyn Monroe, they may have helped aide her in leaving the country to lead the public to believe the Kennedy's were more powerful than what they really were.

The pathologist, Dr. Thomas Noguchi, could find no trace of capsules, powder or the typical discoloration caused by Nembutal in Monroe's stomach or intestines, indicating that the drugs that killed her had not been swallowed. If Monroe had taken them over a period of time (which might account for the lack of residue), she would have died before ingesting the amount found in her bloodstream. Monroe was found lying face down. There was also evidence of cyanosis, an indication that death had been very quick. Noguchi asked the toxicologist for examinations of the blood, liver, kidneys, stomach, urine and intestines, which would have revealed exactly how the drugs got into Monroe's system. However, the toxicologist, after examining the blood, did not believe he needed to check other organs, so many of the organs were destroyed without being examined. Noguchi later asked for the samples, but the medical photographs, the slides of those organs that were examined and the examination form showing bruises on the body had disappeared, making it impossible to investigate the cause of death.

The toxicology report shows high levels of Nembutal (38–66 capsules) and chloral hydrate (14–23 tablets) in Monroe's blood. The level found was enough to kill more than 10 people. An examination of the body ruled out intravenous injection as the source of the drugs. Coroner Dr. Theodore Curphey oversaw the full autopsy. Apart from the cause of death as listed on the death certificate, the results were never made public and no record of the findings was kept.

In the final weeks of her life, Marilyn engaged in discussions about future film projects, and firm arrangements were made to continue negotiations on *Something's Got to Give*. Among the projects was a biography of Jean Harlow filmed two years later unsuccessfully with Carroll Baker. Starring roles in Billy Wilder's *Irma la Douce* and *What a Way to Go!* were also discussed; Shirley MacLaine eventually played the roles in both films. Kim Novak replaced her in *Kiss Me, Stupid*, a comedy in which she was to star opposite Dean Martin. A film version of the Broadway musical, *A Tree Grows in Brooklyn*, and an unnamed World War I-themed musical co-starring Gene Kelly were also discussed, but the projects never materialized due to her death.

Her dispute with *Twentieth Century Fox* was resolved, her contract was renewed into a $1 million two-picture deal, and filming of *Something's Got to Give* was scheduled to resume in early fall 1962. Marilyn, having fired her own agent and MCA in 1961, managed her own negotiations as President of *Marilyn Monroe Productions*.

Also on the table was an Italian four-film deal worth 10 million giving her script, director, and co-star approval. Allan "Whitey" Snyder who saw her during the last week of her life, said Marilyn was pleased by the opportunities available to her, and that she "never looked better and was in great spirits".

Chapter 8

Conflicting Statements:
[Source Reference Number (7): *Crimelibrary.com*]

One area of controversy revolves around the time of Marilyn's death.

The last fact in her life that we can be sure of is that around 7:15 p.m. on Saturday night, she talked with Joe DiMaggio Jr. about his romantic involvements and she was very happy, elated even with the fact that Joe was breaking off a relationship with a woman that Marilyn didn't like. Joe confirms her mood.

But then we have Peter Lawford calling within a half an hour. Marilyn has gone from being happy and alert to heavily drugged, making comments that could be construed as suicidal. Peter Lawford was so panicked that he called his friend, Milt Ebbins, who convinced Marilyn's lawyer, Milton Rudin, to call Marilyn's house to see if she was okay.

Milton Rudin claims that he called the house around 8:30 p.m. and asked Eunice to check on Marilyn. Eunice said that she checked and Marilyn was fine. Peter Lawford wasn't satisfied so he called his friend,

Joe Naar, around 11 p.m. Joe Naar lived close to Marilyn and agreed to go over and make sure that Marilyn had not overdosed. Just as Joe Naar was getting ready to leave his home, he got a call from Milton Rudin telling not to go out — that Marilyn had been given a sedative by Dr. Greenson.

Two other friends of Marilyn said that they spoke with Marilyn during a time period that Peter Lawford was convinced that Marilyn was heavily drugged and possibly dying from an overdose.

When Marilyn's body was taken to the mortuary Sunday morning between 5:30 and 6:00 a.m., he noticed that "rigor mortis was advanced" and estimated that she had died between 9:30 and 11:30 Saturday night.

Arthur Jacobs, Marilyn's publicist, had been told of Marilyn's death around 10:00 to 10:30 Saturday night and had to leave a concert to deal with the press issues.

Eunice, however, claimed that she woke up around 3 a.m., saw a light under Marilyn's bedroom door (which later proved impossible because of deep-pile carpeting), found the door locked (also impossible since there was no functional lock on the door) and called Dr. Greenson. Dr. Greenson came to the house, got into the bedroom and around 3: 50 a.m. declared that Marilyn was dead.

The events that occurred between 9:30 and 10:30 p.m. remain a mystery. However, evidence suggests that sometime during that unaccounted hour Marilyn died. Based on recent testimony by acquaintances and people involved with the events surrounding the alleged suicide, Anthony Summers placed the time of Marilyn's death somewhere within that time frame that evening. Testimony by four of Marilyn's friends supports this theory.

Another investigative report, Donald Wolfe reports that Eunice and son-in-law Norman Jeffries were at Marilyn's house during the night of her death. The two had conflicting stories concerning the events that took place that evening. Jeffries claimed that between 9:30 and 10.00 p.m., Robert Kennedy and two unknown men came to Marilyn's door and ordered them to leave the house. According to Jeffries, they went to a neighbor's home and waited until the men left around 10:30 p.m. When they returned home, Jeffries stated that he saw Marilyn laying face down, naked in her bed and holding what appeared to be a phone.

Jeffries said that Marilyn looked as if she were dead. Eunice allegedly called for an ambulance and then called Dr. Greenson. Donald Wolfe states that Eunice's son-in-law Norman Jeffries saw Peter Lawford and Pat Newcomb arrive at the house too. They were in a state of shock and hysterical. A former ambulance driver named Ken Hunter told an investigator for the district attorney that he arrived at Marilyn's home "in the early morning hours" following the discovery of her body. The ambulance company chief also told the investigator that Marilyn was in fact in a coma when the ambulance arrived, due to an overdose of sleeping pills. He claimed that she was taken to Santa Monica Hospital, where she passed away. Then Marilyn's body was returned to her home in order to facilitate the ongoing cover-up.

Another witness account supported Eunice's son-in-law Norman Jeffries' story, but it was never included in the records of the investigation into Marilyn's death. Elizabeth Pollard, a neighbor of Marilyn's, told police that she saw Robert Kennedy with two unidentified men approach Marilyn's house at about 6 or 7 p.m. One of the unidentified men was carrying a black medical case.

According to Donald Wolfe, the above story was discredited by police and omitted from the investigation because they claimed her story was an "aberration." If it was an aberration, it was one seen by several people.

Eunice Murray sure had a lot of influence of the neighbors of Marilyn Monroe.

Coroner Curphey had based his determination that Marilyn had committed suicide by the amount of sedatives in her body, the presence of prescription bottles for the sedatives, the absence of signs of foul play, her previous suicide attempts, and the opinion of Dr. Greenson.

This opinion, however, was not shared by some key forensic experts who argued that there were no traces of Nembutal in her stomach or intestinal tract. Also, there should have been specific crystals and evidence of the yellow capsules in which Nembutal is packaged. Not only were there no capsule parts, there was no yellow dye in her stomach.

Marilyn's blood count, "there were 8 milligrams of chloral hydrate and four and a half milligrams of Nembutal, but in her liver there was a count of thirteen milligrams, a much higher concentration of Nembutal...The ratio of Nembutal found in the blood compared to that in the liver suggested...that Marilyn lived for many hours after the ingestion of that drug...This means that while Marilyn was alive and mobile, throughout the day, the process of metabolizing the Nembutal she had taken had reached the liver and was beginning the process of excretion...The barbituates were absorbed over a period of not minutes but hours...This report is consistent with what Dr. Greenson himself called her 'somehat drugged' condition."

The idea of an injection of barbiturates was also implausible for two reasons: there were no needle marks found on her body after very close examination, plus an injection of such a high dosage of barbiturates would have caused immediate death, leaving clear bruising.

One possible explanation that was consistent with physical evidence was that the drugs were administered in an enema, which would account for the "abnormal, anomalous discoloration of the colon."

If Marilyn did die of a rectally administered overdose of drugs, it makes the concept of suicide a bit ludicrous and opens up one other possibility: Murder.

Chapter 9

A Discovery [Source Reference Number (10)]

In the wee hours of the morning of August 5, 1962, green police sergeant, Jack Clemmons, would receive a phone call from Dr. Hyman Engelberg that Marilyn Monroe had died from an overdose of pills. After personally driving out to the modest home in Brentwood, Sgt, Clemmons would find Dr. Engleberg accompanied by Eunice and at least one other individual who all led him to Marilyn's bedroom. He saw Marilyn's nude body sprawled face down and positioned diagonally across her bed, her left hand touching the telephone on the nightstand. Next to the telephone were several (some reports say as many as 10-14) empty prescription pill bottles including one that contained several capsules of Nembutal and chloral hydrate (remember this for later.) A more thorough examination failed to turn up a glass that might have been used for water to help down the pills. Upon inquiring about the bathroom, Eunice informed Sgt, Clemmons it was out of order and had no running water. Another curious observation was made by Sgt. Clemmons when he noticed that Eunice had been doing laundry and general tidying up around the house. When questioned, Eunice said that she knew the coroner would eventually come and rope off the house for crime scene investigation, so she wanted the place to look nice.

Sgt. Clemmons noticed that Marilyn's body was in an advanced state of rigor mortis which meant it had been dead for several hours. Upon further questioning, it was revealed by Eunice that she noticed Marilyn's locked door sometime after midnight. Upon receiving no answer after several knocks, Eunice would become concerned and called Dr. Engleberg who was subsequently unable to arouse Marilyn by knocking on the door. The pair would then go around outside and peek in through her window. Only after breaking the window with a fireplace poker were they able to gain entry into Marilyn's bedroom. But it was too late. The 36 year-old actress was already dead. Four hours had passed before Eunice contacted the authorities. I'm not implicating anyone here, but that's way more time than would be necessary to call Marilyn's studios and some of her business associates, as Eunice claimed. I'm just saying!

Marilyn's body was taken to Westwood Village Mortuary and the house was sealed and placed under guard for further investigation.

Chapter 10

Aftermath

The Death of Marilyn Monroe, by Frank Wilkins:

The 36 year-old actress was already dead. Four hours had passed before Eunice contacted the authorities. I'm not implicating anyone here, but that's way more time than would be necessary to call Marilyn's studios and some of her business associates, as Eunice claimed. I'm just saying!

It might also be worthy of mention that Mrs, Eunice Murray, Marilyn's housekeeper had been fired earlier in the day of Marilyn's death. I'm just stating the facts here. Not trying to implicate anyone.

Los Angeles Times staff writer, Robert W. Welkos's, New Chapter in the Mystery of Marilyn: Her Own Words?, written in August 5th, 2005:

In the tapes, Monroe heaps praise on Kennedy, and there is no suggestion that the two were ever lovers. "This man is going to change our country," she says of JFK, adding, "He will transform America today like FDR did in the '30s."

Police did not interview Peter Lawford until 1975, when he talked officially of his phone calls with her on the final night. That confidential police file was made public last week by Police Chief Daryl F. Gates. In 1982, Peter Lawford told the district attorney that he learned of Monroe's death at 1:30 a.m. and was positive about the time because he looked at a bedside clock after receiving the phone call from his manager.

In his 1984 interview with The Times, Peter Lawford recounted again what happened that night.

Peter Lawford said he told Monroe that night that "five or six" people were coming over to play poker at his beach house.

'I Just Don't Feel Well,' he claims Marilyn replied.

"It was about 6 or half-past 6 and she said to me, 'Peter, I don't think I'm going to make it tonight because I just don't feel well.'

I said, 'Oh, Marilyn, come on.' It was starting to rain. I said, 'Come on down, you can go home early. Call me back. Dinner won't be until 8 or 8:30.'

She said, 'OK, I'll call you back.' So she rang back. I could hear the depression really moving in on her. She said, 'I really don't think I can come down tonight.' "

Peter Lawford said she replied: "Will you say goodby to Pat, and to Jack and to yourself, because you're a nice guy."

Peter Lawford said he tried to verbally slap Monroe, saying, "Hey, Marilyn, what is that.? Come on now!"

She said, 'You've all been so nice to me.' He said, 'Marilyn!'

"I started to really get angry and frightened," he recalled. "

She said: 'I'll see. I'll see.' And she hung up. . . .

I tried to ring her back and it was busy. It was busy, busy, busy for an hour and a half. Now, to this day, I've lived with this. I should have got into my car and gone straight to her house. I didn't do it." Peter Lawford relives.

At this point in the interview, Peter Lawford broke down and cried.

He said he telephoned his manager, Milton Ebbins, and asked him to contact psychiatrist Dr. Greenson and Milton (Mickey) Rudin, Monroe's attorney, and have them check on her because he had a "bad feeling."

"I went to dinner," he continued. "My head wasn't there. I was worrying about it. Don't ask me why I didn't get up and go. I kept rationalizing, 'No, she's not going to do that,' so I called Milton Ebbins back about 9:30 and he was out. He rang me between 11 and 12 (midnight). He said, 'I finally got hold of Micky Rudin, who was getting hold of Dr. Greenson.' He said, 'They're on their way over there.'"

Milton Ebbins told The Times that "Micky Rudin called me from the house and told me they'd just broken in and found the body."

Micky Rudin was interviewed briefly in 1962 by Detective Byron but said only that he telephoned housekeeper Murray at 9 p.m. and asked her if Monroe was all right. Told that she was, Micky Rudin said he dismissed the possibility of anything further being wrong. Micky Rudin, who was the psychiatrist's Dr. Greenson's brother-in-law, has remained silent on the case ever since.

Robert Kennedy had attended a meeting of the American Bar Association. in San Francisco that weekend and then, according to official reports, went with his wife and children to the home of friends on a farm in Gilroy, California.

Carroll and his investigator, Alan Tomich, found no evidence in 1982 that Kennedy was in Los Angeles that day in 1962.

Chapter 11

Theory & Analysis

When Eunice Murray met Marilyn Monroe almost two years earlier, her life was in a downward tailspin. Now, it seemed, she was heading back up, getting back on track. She was being offered movie contracts again, under her own production company name, her friendships had expanded beyond Hollywood and brimmed the political arena all the way up to the President of the United States, himself. I guess sex really can buy you anything you want. Eunice felt she wasn't needed anymore. Eunice was right. Not only was Eunice Murray *not needed* anymore, Marilyn *did not want* her around anymore either.

Marilyn had given Eunice a pink slip terminating her employment with her two weeks prior, as well as reminded her she was fired from Marilyn Monroe's household as her personal housekeeper and "flunkie," more than once throughout the day Marilyn died on August 4th, 1962, and Eunice had had enough.

Many theories site the fact that Marilyn knew too much and had to be killed because of it. Someone did know too much and needed to be terminated because of it: Eunice Murray. Eunice Murray knew too much about Marilyn Monroe …… all of the men she had sex with; had to listen to her have sex with them, top quality men; had to watch has her life slowly took an upswing, indicating a no longer need for Eunice Murray or Dr. Ralph Greenson.

Taking advantage of the Chloral Hydrate Eunice had seen Dr. Ralph Greenson administer to Marilyn earlier in the day causing her slowly to slip into a "drugged-out" state, Eunice decided to make her move. She also remembered all the news clips she saw on television and read in the newspapers that stated Marilyn had attempted to kill herself several times in the past by dumping an entire bottle of sleeping pills down her throat.

Upon listening to Marilyn talking to Peter Lawford, seeing the Chloral Hydrate was rendering Marilyn unable to talk in a comprehensible manner……. Eunice Murray started the quick process of murdering Marilyn Monroe. Before she even had a chance to hang up the telephone, Eunice Murray took a handful of Marilyn Monroe's "sleeping pills," as much as her evil hearted hand could hold, and shoved them up Marilyn Monroe's rectum with her entire fist, released the pills by opening her hand up, and retracted her entire now open hand. The entire process was probably executed in less than one minute's time.

Eunice Murray hung the receiver to the phone up, and left Marilyn's bedroom. It was quick and fast. So fast Marilyn didn't even have a chance to think or react. Except Marilyn, the strong person that she was, made one last attempt to save her own life, picked up the phone to call .... only she will ever know to who to tell that person one final last good-bye before she passed away to the great beyond.

Dr. Ralph Greenson, so convinced no one in the entire world would believe Eunice Murray acted alone, when he and Dr. Hyman Engelberg figured out what Eunice Murray had done when they talked to each other alone in Marilyn Monroe's bedroom after they broke her window to get in, decided to help cover up what Eunice had done, prior to the police arriving.

Milton A. "Mickey" Rudin, Marilyn Monroe's attorney as well as Dr. Ralph Greenson's brother-in-law, knew what Eunice Murray had done as well, but never spoke to anyone about it ever, after August 5th, 1962. I guess it's easy for trained lawyers to keep quiet about things that need not be talked about.

I'm not even sure they told Eunice they knew what she had done: Shoved a full bottle of Marilyn Monroe's barbiturates up her rectum through her anus, and then left the room leaving her to die ……. alone.

Crime breads romance. People love to add romance to crime. It seems to soften the blow a bit, that final fatal blow that everyone knows is coming their way, they just put it off as long as possible. The Kennedy's did not kill Marilyn Monroe or even considered it. Marilyn had too many other high profile sexual relationships: This one was no different than the others. And John F. Kennedy had too many other high profile women he had been engaging in sexually with, as well.

Of course, the Kennedy's probably encouraged the public at large to think they had something to do with Marilyn's death. It gives them more power, and people are attracted to power, good or evil power. If people think the Kennedy's killed Marilyn Monroe, just because she had sex with Robert or John, or both, then that is a lot of power built up behind those thick political walls the Kennedy's liked to live their lives in, or at least think they can , and politicians will take all the power they can possibly get: After all, it's all about getting the next vote, right?

References

(1) http://www.fanpop.com/clubs/marilyn-monroe/images/979553/title/marilyn-wallpaper

(2) http://famous-wallpapers.com/marilyn-monroe-wallpaper/

(3) http://news.yahoo.com/photos/undated-publicity-photo-courtesy-running-press-marilyn-monroe-photo

(4) http://www.arts-wallpapers.com/classic_celebrity/marilyn_monroe_wallpapers.htm

(5) http://www.dumpaday.com/random-pictures/marilyn-monroe-30-amazing-photos/

(6) http://www.nydailynews.com/entertainment/marilyn-monroe-50th-anniversary-death-gallery-1.1128658?pmSlide=1.1128626

(7) http://www.crimelibrary.com/notorious_murders/celebrity/marilyn_monroe/index.html

(8) http://en.wikipedia.org/wiki/Death_of_Marilyn_Monroe

(9) http://www.biography.com/people/marilyn-monroe-9412123/videos/marilyn-monroe-death-2263052289

(10) http://www.franksreelreviews.com/shorttakes/marilynmonroe.htm

(11) http://english.pravda.ru/society/stories/03-07-2013/125016-marilyn_monroe_death-0/

(12) http://latimesblogs.latimes.com/lanow/2012/12/fbi-examined-theories-about-marilyn-monroes-death-papers-show.html

(13) http://articles.latimes.com/2005/aug/05/entertainment/et-marilyn5/3

(14) http://en.wikipedia.org/wiki/Peter_Lawford

(15) http://en.wikipedia.org/wiki/The_Kennedys_(miniseries)

(16) http://en.wikipedia.org/wiki/Marilyn_Monroe

(17) http://www.amazon.com/Fragments-Poems-Intimate-Notes-Letters/dp/0374533784/ref=sr_1_3?ie=UTF8&qid=1411435866&sr=8-3&keywords=fragments#reader_0374533784

(18)   http://en.wikipedia.org/wiki/Joe_DiMaggio

(19)   http://en.wikipedia.org/wiki/Arthur_Miller

(20)   http://en.wikipedia.org/wiki/Joseph_P._Kennedy,_Sr.

(21)   http://www.historyplace.com/speeches/edward.htm

Postscript

*In her eyes, and in mine,
her career was just beginning....
She had a luminous quality.
A combination of wistfulness, radiance,
and yearning that set her apart
and made everyone wish to be part of it —
to share in the childish naiveté
which was at once so shy and yet so vibrant.*

~Lee Strasberg, *her acting teacher, and the person she left all of her personal belongings to in her will*

About the Author

Gwendolyn Olmsted, MBA, the former Washington DC microbiologist and research scientist, who conducted graduate level research at major universities as well as United States federal governmental facilities, moved to Florida in 2010. She has a Bachelor's and Master's degree in Business Finance, as well as a second Bachelor's and Master's degree in Environmental Sciences & Sustainability from both private and public universities. Ms. Olmsted has also been employed by the United States Air Force in the early 1990's, stationed in the United Kingdom as well as other locations unable to be disclosed, with an Honorable Discharge. Married to a corporate Washington DC attorney in 2007, with children, Gwendolyn now writes stories from the Docu-Eroticamentary, Investigative True Crime, Biographical, Documentary, and Investigative Journalism genres.

CPSIA information can be obtained at www.ICGtesting.com
Printed in the USA
LVOW10s1924101215

466287LV00033B/939/P